The Art of Reprogramming the Mindset
Quentin aka "qdaboss"
Brown

The Art of Reprogramming the Mindset©

Quentin aka "qdaboss" Brown

May 16, 2021

Library of Congress: 1-11509941711

ISBN: 978-17358122-5-0

Printed USA

Chloe Arts and Publishing, LLC
Write the vision make it plain. Habakkuk 2:2

TABLE OF CONTENTS

FOREWORD

It is known that Halley's comet orbits the earth every seventy-five years, which means that an individual may only see it once in their lifetime. I think of Que like our version of Halley's comet. He has the profound ability to take complex ideas and make them easy to understand. In this book, you will dive into the intricate mind of Que. He never ceases to amaze me. The fact that he was able to put his thoughts into this book testifies to the kind of person Que is. His burden for our community is worthy of applause. The information you will get from this book is priceless. Most people in this world seek to improve it for themselves, and some make it better for others. Que falls into the latter group.

While many seek ways to exploit our culture and community, Que has invested his time and money into giving back to the places that raised him. His street knowledge and book knowledge make him a prophet of the pavement, clearing the way to success and opening the doors for others to be what they are created to be. We need more books like these, and I would even dare to say that we need more people like Que in this world.

The pathway to success is not an easy road. It comes with obstacles, challenges, and pitfalls along the way. With a book like this, you will have a head start a blueprint to navigate through these challenges.

Stay encouraged, change the game, and change the world.

-   Pastor Jaime Kowlessar

ACKNOWLEDGMENTS

I would be remiss if I didn't preface this book with a heartfelt gracious appreciation to my village of supporters. Before I get into my human appreciation, I first must thank God for what He has done for me, and continues to do for me, and will always do for me. The journey wasn't always easy, but I appreciate every lesson you've so powerfully taught me along the way. Thank you for developing a greater me than I could even begin to imagine. Now, to name just a few of my villagers, I must first acknowledge a woman who has been a tower of strength to me, pushed me beyond my limits, and supported me. Immensely. Mom, you taught me to chase my dreams and never give up. Your strength has motivated me to become the strong man many witnesses today. Mom, from the bottom of my heart—THANK YOU. To my older brother Jeffrey Huffman—thank you for being my biggest supporter. You've always displayed immense honesty and are always straight forward with me.

You called me out and addressed my behavior on many occasions, which fashioned and molded me. Thank you. Hazel Brown—my grandmother—thank you for being so impactful in my life and always being positive regardless of the situation. My best friend Gino always provoked me to see that there is more to life, and you've stuck by me no matter what. For that, thank you. Aliesha Grange—you have been a force in my life, always supportive and always pushing me to climb to even higher levels. Your selflessness has always blown my mind. I just want to let you know— sky's the limit—there is nothing we can't achieve together. My children—Nathaniel, Madison and Quinn Brown—you are my motivation. I will always push myself to be a better version of myself and to be the best father and role model I can ever be for you guys.

Tony and Farrah—my brother and sister from another mother—thank you for all your support and sharing a different perspective with me always. My siblings—

Marlon, Shaquille, Dion, and Daijana—it's family over everything. My business partner and friend—Kenneth Pierre Louis—blood couldn't make us any more family than we are.

To Andre Denoon and Esther Cummings, thank you for pushing me to publish this book thereby allowing me to become a published author. To my team Tyler, Kinsey, Sam, Boss Dre, Vivian, Chrys and Miriam Mars—thank you for supporting and helping me promote my brand—qdaboss.

To my mentors, Sean Ramalho, Gary Fyffe—you guys truly inspire me on a whole other level. To Richard Gresio, I've been blessed to have a friend for my lawyer. My empowered dynasty family—thank you for always being my greatest support. Let's keep gaining and building. Dr. Stephen Carryl, thank you for all your support. To my Pastor Jaime Kowlessar, thank you for believing in me and seeing the great in me.

To all the people who supported me always—thank you for pushing me, supporting me, and always helping support any platform I've chosen to stand on.

God bless you all.

INTRODUCTION

This book is a compilation of thoughts and observations I have had based on my life experiences. Plain and simple, our mindset is the primary focus. In society today, many issues and problems persist among all communities and nationalities. One of the major identifiable issues or problems is mindset. Mindsets determine results. Results are the conclusion of one's mindset.

Mental programming is a reflection of people's mindset. In most cases, one will become the product of the way they program their mindset. The program of a mindset determines how one speaks about themselves, how they think about themselves, how they conduct themselves, and how they represent themselves. Some people have better results than others, and this can be based on mental programming. To change mindsets, one must reprogram the mindset.

One question that has always plagued my mind is why some people have great results and massive success, while others fail or remain at a stagnant position in life. The answer I arrived at is based on the specific formulas needed to navigate life, and how varying people embrace those formulas. In order to achieve great success and be a person of influence one must, at some point in life, break the program curse. To do so, one must reprogram their mindset. Reprogramming will force a person to educate themselves, make sacrifices, and work hard in order to achieve life's goals.

This book presents many facets of reprogramming the mindset in order to achieve financial freedom, massive success, and just basic happiness in life.

I pray and hope that after reading this book, many people from all walks of life will reprogram their mindsets, and in so doing, free generations to come from the programmer's curse.

3

Chapter 1
Group Economics
Discussion on the pros of group economics verses the myth of individual success

Let's talk about Group Economics. Group Economics is essentially a group of people with common economic interests. Common economic interests drive these people to actively pursue that interest, so that they can create a secure economy for all participants in the group economic structure. People who join together grow ten times faster economically than the people doing it alone. Let's examine this analogy— you have four friends sitting in a car; one friend's job is the driver, the second friend gives directions, while the third and fourth friends are responsible for the finances of the trip. They have decided they will be driving from New York to California. If none of these friends can do their jobs, they will never get to California. If they each decide to do this trip alone, it will be more costly and take a much longer time to get there versus the four of them doing it together. Applying this concept to life would be to grow as a team with a team. Individuals win awards but teams win championships. Group economics allows communities to be built, and community members to control the productivity and narrative of the environment. The ultimate goal is growth, and the fastest way to grow is teamwork. The main benefit of group economics is to strengthen your community by ensuring that the money is cycling through the community multiple times before it leaves. When money remains within a community, it allows businesses and residents to direct that money so that a profit is seen.

Group economics dictates that communities be built and controls the productivity and narrative of the environment. The ultimate goal is to grow, and the fastest way to grow is teamwork. The main benefit of group economics is to strengthen your community by ensuring that the money is cycling through the community multiple times before it leaves. When money stays in the community, it allows businesses, residents, and investors to direct that money into neighborhood schools, parks, and capital improvements of various assets, thus increasing the value of the community as a whole.

A few ways to make a difference are by grouping together to start more businesses and hire people on the same mission. Create trust funds for children and most of all improve the community as a whole while totally understanding finance and economics. Many people fall short on executing life-changing measures, such as accumulating wealth, being better prepared for retirement, and building up savings. Group economics allows the average to not be so average anymore by joining forces with others.

Joining forces with like-minded individuals takes away the feeling of being average. The reason most people fail is because they really don't understand the powers in unification. Many people believe they'll become wealthy by doing things alone. They have a mogul mentality, an instant gratification mentality. A mentality that says, "I'm going to do it alone." A "me, me, me" mentality. This is why most people fail. Society is not designed to allow people to win alone. When you see people winning alone, it's because they are not exposing their team members or partners. If we traded home boys, home girls, my 'bros' and my 'homies' for business partners, business acquaintances, and business associates, we'd be more successful; it would catapult us as a people to another level. These are people who share similar goals and interests. When you are surrounded by a group of people who share your common interests and goals, it is easy to win. Most people fail because they spend a lot of their time navigating the deep waters of success alone. There are lots of failures in that water of success. If we're all in a boat using our abilities to navigate the waters together, then we have higher chances of achieving success. It becomes easy to change positioning because everyone is on the same page. For example, if in a group of ten people, everyone brings $100,000 dollars, that becomes a million dollars versus one person struggling with $100,000 and trying to be successful.

There is now a major setup going on—the employee mentality. You are programmed to think like an employee, not an employer. You see yourself as a worker, not the boss. Therefore, people only see themselves as working and never a boss. At the end of the day, your mindset is taught to be an employee. You can't ever reach the magnitude of who you should be at the employee mindset. This, of course, has to do with a mentality—a mindset. Society teaches these programs. The mind is like a computer, and is programmed to think that way. Therefore, we need to reset our minds to produce new information. Failure is not because a person is dumb, but because of a distorted mindset—as long as I'm doing my thing, I'm good. Speeding up the process of success has to do with a group of like-minded people. People with shared goals and common interests. Unification and group economics are what allows us to speed up the process of success. Do not spend your time on foolish conversations, and foolish things. When you realize you are your own enemy, you realize you have to make better decisions so that you can succeed.

There is another popular term for pooling economics, and it's called crowd funding. This is a method of raising capital through the collective efforts of friends, family, customers, and individual investors. Learning the whole goal is to teach teamwork. When we truly understand this concept, teamwork will be embraced even more. Group economics is the idea that allows us to work together and eliminate selfish ways.

There is no "I" in team and no "me" in together. We cannot blame others. We have to see that our purpose and destiny is our responsibility. Make decisions that will bring you closer to success. Here is an analogy: imagine a boat in the middle of the ocean, but the boat is full of holes. One can plug the holes in the boat to prevent water from entering the boat. Our plan of success can be like a boat with holes. How do you fix your holes? By making effective decisions. Following the formula of losers makes it difficult to win. If the hole causing you to sink consists of second guessing yourself, plug that hole and plug the fear of failure. Plug excuses, poor mentality, and arrogance. Plug your distrust, unwillingness to work with others, and victimization. Change your mindset.

Manifestation never works alone. We can manifest forever, but we must work. Faith without works is dead. It is impossible to be successful if you're not sacrificing, working hard, and being accountable. Your failures are based on your decisions and actions. Your failures are not to be blamed on anything or anyone else. You will be much more effective if you choose to be part of a group, follow success, be accountable, and not attempt to do it all alone... Group economics versus the 'alone' distorted mentality.

Chapter 2
Building Generational Wealth

Selfishness has become visible in today's culture. This selfishness even includes parents. Parents are no longer raising and guiding their children, establishing them at the magnitude of what they could be.

I will talk about the New York area, as that's where I'm familiar with. In New York, my grandfather could have purchased a house and paid $100,000. If my father purchased that same house, he would pay $300,000. My generation seeking to purchase that same house will pay anywhere from $400,000 to $500,000. My son will pay $700,000 to $800,000. Inflation is responsible for this phenomenon. Therefore, parents should establish their children by leaving these properties to them, instead of selling them to make a profit. However, parents aren't establishing their children. This puts the next generation ahead of the curve. It makes sense to establish the children.

Real estate and life insurance should be left for the next generation. Parents should leave a legacy for their children. People in this generation are living for themselves and do not care about the future or generations after them. Your legacy is what you leave behind. Most people don't care about their legacy, so they live selfishly and in doing so, prevent the building of generational wealth.

My theory is this: you establish your children by investing in them, therefore your children are more advanced than you. Children should be our top priority. Children should alert us to the fact that an investment must be made in them. As a people we make the same economical mistakes because we think selfishly. Generational wealth is not created in one generation; it is created over generations to come. We cannot keep chasing the logic of money and just money. Money is a tool; we overvalue money as we think it will take away problems or make us happy. Money can give you freedom. If I build an empire, where I can make $25,000 a year, then my objective is to teach my children how to sustain that. Therefore, my children will inherit $25,000 a year minimum. But we are not embracing that thought process. Our culture is simply selfish. I've been observing parents attempting to live rich by wasting their resources to keep up with a 'look' opposed to reality.

Generational wealth is obtained by teaching the next generation to be the successor of what you have created. You cannot inherit a career job or a degree. People tend to brag about their degrees and careers but you cannot inherit that. Your objective should be to leave your children something that is sustainable. When the focus comes off you and on to the children, the goals change and shift. You then make decisions to put your children and your family in a better position. If you give your family a jump start on life, they can defy the odds; they can beat the odds because they've been equipped. The average person inherits great debt versus inheriting a great start to a great life. The sad part is families take reverse mortgages out and lose the assets they acquire. Sometimes we have to be willing to give away our own lives so our future generations can live better lives. The entire goal is to set your family up to the point that they are doing better than you economically.

The goal should be to live through your children by creating generational wealth. Your children shouldn't know struggle, economic struggle, like you did. The goal is to ensure they're more advanced than you are. You have the ability to determine that and to create generational wealth to prevent that. The point is not to score two points in the game of life, it's to win a championship. The championship is generational wealth.

I say this every day: your mindset and perception is everything. It's not just about living in a good area, it is about living in better areas so they can think differently. We must work on the perception of your children and their mindset. Generational wealth is investing in children and family. Worry more about your last names; they mean more than your first name. Your last name determines the future and trajectory of your family. Teach your children to be greater than you were. Teach your children to want more and how to sustain an empire. There are so many foreclosures because children weren't taught how to sustain these things. One of the forbidden conversations in homes is about money. We tend to think children will just figure it out. They will not. We are required to discuss money, discuss credit, and discuss financial principles. Credit is never taught, it's not spoken about, so it's foreign to them. As a result, we have a generation of people who don't know better. It's taught now where it's systematic.

It has to be about your children, not you. My time and energy are invested into my children. Understanding how important your children—your legacy—will propel you to build generational wealth so their lives are better. Your children should be in a better position than you, and your grandchildren in a better position than your children. Teaching them to be better—teaching them to build wealth focuses on a mindset. It's all about the way you think. Understanding money is a mindset. The easy "come ups" and "get rich" ploys are not reality. You have to build brick by brick.

That generational wealth may not be built in your generation, it may be in the next generation or the one after that. But have the understanding that your last name is the value, thinking how your family can be greater that's how you win. The grandfather works hard, the son should come along and take it further, the grandson even further. That's how we build generational wealth. If I bought a house and paid twenty-five years into the mortgage, I could leave it to my son with just five years of payment. I should get as far into the mortgage as I can so that my son has only a small amount of payment. However, the value of the property has gone up since I bought it. So, he gains on the value of that property. As stated earlier, when a grandfather buys for a small value, the next generation buys value up and the other generations to follow will earn from the increase in property value. It is key to teach our kids about credit, how to be greater, and how to be financially mature. It's about maturity when it comes to finances. Finances mature. If your child is saying it's only a dollar, that means you're failing your children. Your children should be taught how to respect money. When a person is broke, they don't respect money. Frugal people understand money. It takes money to make money. Generational wealth is not obtained in one generation, it happens over time, but somebody has to get the ball rolling. Generational wealth is the willingness to sacrifice oneself for the next generation.

Most people aren't born with a silver spoon, nor are they born into wealth. It is ultimately the sacrifices that the generations that came before you which allowed you to be able to acquire an amount of wealth. Those generations before you toiled and sacrificed to allow for this acquisition we now enjoy. This wealth creates a lifestyle and privileges for the next generation wherein they are given a fruitful head start into creating their own wealth. The mindset of the wealthy is to ensure that they leave the next generation in a position to create and sustain a wealthy lifestyle for themselves. It must be stated that there is a difference between generational wealth and personal wealth. Generational wealth is a concept where a family streams significant amounts of assets onto a future generation. A family's generational wealth, or commonly known as a family fortune, is derived from years of hard work and sacrifice. The family members starting to build generational wealth are thinking about generations to come, not necessarily the present generation. Their thought process is beyond themselves and their personal acquisitions of wealth.

In order to ensure that our future generations to come are comfortably sustained with a flow of wealth, we must work and sacrifice to ensure this is a reality for them. Personal wealth, acquiring wealth for the now to benefit me, will never ensure that this happens.

Empower your mind, empower your life—you control your destiny.

Chapter 3
What is a Father?

A father is defined as a person who treats with protective care; is involved; behaves responsibly; is emotionally engaged; is physically available; provides financial support and is influential in a child's raising decisions. This is what a father is.

A lot of people don't know how to be a father. I personally grew up without my father. There is a difference between father and dad. Father is the name that appears on every birth certificate. A Dad is the man who fulfills the above definition above and beyond. We need more dads than fathers.

Protective care—a man who is physically strong or masculine or fights for your child does not mean they're a father. Fatherhood is the willingness to say to yourself whatever my child needs, I'll make sure the need is met. A lot of people tend to believe being physically strong and fighting for your child makes you a father. To me, protective care is the willingness to ensure that your child has whatever it needs. A lot of kids are exposed to activities that they shouldn't be exposed to because there is no structure at home. The examples of fathers we're seeing is horrifying. A lot of fathers do not take it as a real experience or hold themselves responsible. My child has to know I'm their father and will sacrifice myself for my child. By any means, I will protect them.

Being involved—children are raising themselves. They are doing so via social media, video games, etc. Fathers are no longer playing ball with kids in the backyard. No one is involved with their kids. Kids are being shown at an early age poor examples of what it means to be a father. Boys think they're adults because they're having sex. Their father never put them in their place; the boys eventually outgrow a mother's verbal lashing or any kind of discipline because he's strong and he's a man. A sixteen-year-old having sex

22

thinks they're a man because no father showed him how to be a child. A boy thinks he's a man because he's intimate with a female, but no one is showing him how to navigate life as a man. I am guilty of this myself. I myself thought I was a man before I became a man. My inconsistencies were evident when I picked and chose what I wanted to be a man. I wanted to be a grown man but then I wanted to go back to a child stage when things got overwhelming. Unfortunately, there is no turning back; there's no tucking of tail between legs and running back. But a man would have to show a boy how to handle these things. I will go on the record and say this: I've noticed that most men will argue with a woman for three hours. That is a female trait, but I'm noticing more and more that men are doing it. That's happening because a lot of men are growing up with women and learning from women because men are not involved. They're learning how to adapt to the feminine side. If a real man was there, he'd show that boy/man that's not the way. You say your piece and you keep moving. When a man is involved, he is holding another boy or man accountable. That man being developed will see the consistencies of the man involved. Becoming a man will be shown to him. That's what being involved does for a boy transitioning into manhood. When a man is involved, he will hold the hand of the developing boy and will teach and show how to be a man.

Behaving responsibly—too many kids see too many wrong things. A boy witnessing his father being a womanizer is not seeing an example of a man committed to one woman. Men, hold yourself accountable; hold yourself responsible and lead by example. Do not tell the children "Don't curse" while you curse at them. Being responsible is an action. It defines who you are. Men, don't let your sons see you involved with more than one woman. I myself am guilty of that. It is not acceptable; you are taking away his understanding of monogamy. In the long run he will not respect marriage or commitment. We are behaving like children and becoming a contradiction. I'm telling him how to behave but I behave differently. Examples include, save your money while I spend mine; don't curse while I curse; respect the opposite sex while I'm not. Being responsible is an action. It defines who you are as a man.

Be emotionally engaged. This is one of my favorite topics as far as fatherhood. One day my son walked into one of my establishments. In front of a group of men, I asked him to give me a hug. The first thing he did was to look around the room. Doing so, he disengaged with my request, because he was looking at all the men there and thinking he'd have to give me a hug in front of all of them. He was more worried with how he'd be viewed because he's giving his dad a hug in a room filled with men. So, I again asked for a hug, he looked at me again. I then said, "What's the problem? You're thinking about what others are thinking about you." Clearly that was the case. I then realized I have to teach my son to be emotionally sound in any setting. Where, if his father needs a hug, he is not concerned about what the perception of the room is. You have to normalize certain behaviors. Men have feelings. As fathers, it's our job to show our children that even though we are very masculine and strong and have very muscular bodies, we're *still* human. My child should know dad can cry and be frustrated because he's human. Showing feelings doesn't mean weakness. Our children, more so our sons, are very disengaged when it comes to expressing emotions. They have to be taught that it's ok to seek guidance, it's okay to want someone to talk to, to have a therapist. Our boys have to be taught how to express themselves. However, we have a lot of men who have not yet learned or mastered how to express themselves. They express themselves with anger and yelling and physicality and fighting and this is what is considered to be a man. A man should know how to control himself in any setting as a person who is comfortable in his skin. If I can say words to you that means there is emotional distress based on the fact that words make you act or behave a certain way. The reality of understanding the power of emotional engagement is highly important. A child should always have a father who teaches them how to express emotions correctly. Men, teach your sons that a man has feelings; a man is not a robot, he is human.

Being physically available—Sometimes I feel that we believe that we are out working and we work and work and work and that's all that our children need. Quite the opposite, the thing children need the most is our time, is our presence. The thing they remember the most is the time spent. Out of everything, they'll remember time. They don't remember what you bought them, they remember the time when you showed up at games, when dad told me he loves me, when dad showed me he will always be there. A lot of fathers have a disengagement because fathers aren't making sacrifices to spend time with children. A child has to understand that fathers will be there no matter what. It's not only the mom's responsibility to be there, but also the father should be there. For instance, the parent-teachers conference—Dad needs to be at all activities. I understand bills exist. I get it, but the child has to know of your presence and understand that you care. After all, that's their measuring rod for how much you care. When they don't feel your presence, an extreme amount of discomfort, anger, resentment will surface. A lot of males have commitment issues based on the fact that they were never made to feel that dad was there. For me, my dad was never in my life, but my dad and I learnt from each other as adults: my father as an older man and me as a man with children, family, and responsibilities. There was never a moment of learning from my father on how to be a parent. I winged it. I became a parent in my teens; my son is eighteen years younger than me and I was his age when I had him. I had to quickly learn, it's not just about money. The other day I took my son to teach him how to drive. The next day my younger brother told me how my son was bragging about how I took him out to drive. It wasn't about me buying him a car or taking him on a vacation, it was about the time he spent with his father teaching him how to drive. It's deeper than money. Fathers understand, we play a major role in our children's development. Being physically available does a lot for the development of a child because they know you care.

Providing financial support—child support. Fathers are known to curse and fuss about child support. Last time I checked, children have to eat and live, they do not live on thin air. Raising children costs money. Children have needs—men have to understand that. Women have expectations of a father. It should not be her sole job to provide for a child. I think it's wrong that fathers cry about child support. Be more responsible about having sex. We should be fruitful and multiply, and I agree with that statement, however, the woman we'll be fruitful and multiply with, should be the woman we commit ourselves to so that there aren't a bunch of babies hanging out there fatherless. I am guilty, as I had a child out of wedlock, but I was very young. A child growing up in your house has a stronger financial support system than a child growing up in someone else's home because one or two incomes into a home create a more stable financial situation for the child to develop. Men, I beg you, stop making babies with women and then cry about child support. Make a conscious decision that you need to wrap it up. If you are not thinking about a long-term responsibility, then become responsible with your decisions. Children need to be taken care of financially in order to produce a sound, well rounded child.

Having influence on child raising decisions—a lot of women will not respect you if you're inconsistent as a man. A woman will not allow you to make certain decisions about her child if you're inconsistent. She has to know you're going to make the right decisions about her child and be responsible. If a woman isn't confident in your decision making, she will not allow you to choose certain aspects on the raising of her child. And that's human nature. A woman will not allow you to make decisions about her child or on the raising of her child when you are still making a boy type decision. If you're not responsible, she will not allow you to make decisions about her child. Men have to be a consistent force in that child's life. Your child needs to understand what it is to have a father who is consistently there because you provide a high level of security and tell your child you will make sacrifices for them. I truly believe certain decisions we make as fathers have to be held accountable within our decision-making process. Our children start with what we make of ourselves. Don't be mad if you're raising a child you're not proud of. Are you proud of yourself? It starts with being fathers, let us work on our parenting skills. Fatherhood is not just a word, it is a consistent action. Fatherhood means treating with protective care, being involved, behaving responsibly, being emotionally engaged, physically available, providing financial support, and having an influence in your child-raising decisions.

There are many pros to a father being present and actively involved with the raising of a child. The child will, as an adult, make wiser decisions about relationships and finances and generally about their own adult lives. The likelihood of teenage pregnancy is far less when a father is actively involved. Behavioral and emotional difficulties are far less. Teenagers are more likely to attain great educational success and less likely to serve time in prison. A father is extremely necessary in the developmental process of a child. Fathers, we must treat this role as the most serious one we'll ever have and do our best to ensure that our presence and involvement stays on an all-time high. Our children need us desperately in order to be successful adults. Remember, it took two adults to conceive a child, therefore, it will take two adults to effectively raise that child.

Chapter 4
24 Hours

There are twelve months in a year, three hundred sixty-five days in a year, seven days in a week, twenty-four hours in a day, and sixty seconds in a minute. Let's break down the hours in a day. You may sleep for eight hours and work for eight hours. That leaves you with eight hours. In between sleeping and working, you may commute for two hours, prepare for work for one hour, and eat lunch for an hour. This leaves you with five free hours in a day for your children and family. What I'm trying to point out to you is that everyone has the same amount of time. Do not waste your precious time you've been allotted.

No one is special. I truly believe that everyone is born with a gift. Some people are gifted musicians, some gifted athletes, some possess extreme mental toughness, some possess a photographic memory. These are all gifts. Gifts are instilled by God into a person. What makes you special is what you're willing to do with your gifts that others aren't willing to do.

A lot of people need to reprogram their minds. They need to understand what happens in twenty-four hours is dependent on how you use the hours that have been given to you. How you capitalize on every second of every minute of every hour of every day. Twenty-four hours—repeat that phrase when you wake up—all you have is twenty-four hours to get things done within a day. Every second of that time has to be accounted for. If you start breaking down your time, you'll realize that life is short and you don't have as much time as you truly think you have. Reprogram your mind to realize I have to value my time. My time means more than I'm giving it value. No one will feel sorry for you and just hand you things. Every day you wake up, your day should be accounted for.

People waste their time and sleep until 1 p.m. or 2 p.m. then wake up crying about their lives. No reason to cry, stop snoozing the alarm, or choose to keep on sleeping. You can oversleep but when you wake up, you'll realize you wasted a lot of time that is not regained. Break down your day and capitalize on your time in the day. What I do with my time determines how successful I will be. Some of us are sleeping too much. Reprogram your body to get up and win—successful people do not make excuses. Successful people wake up and get up because they have to win. You have decisions to make about your life, sleeping your life away, wasting your twenty-four hours will not allow you to be successful.

Doors may close in your face. That does not mean you give up, you either learn how to kick the door in or find the back door. You may not be where you want to be today, but you have to make sacrifices to get to where you want to be. No one will feel sorry for you. Capitalizing on your twenty-four hours will determine your success.

We make sacrifices, not excuses. We cannot do the same thing every day and think things will change. That is insanity—doing the same thing every day and expecting different results. The people doing well, the ones who built up from the mud, take the path with the most obstacles. These are not the inheritance-type folks, these are the average folks who start from scratch and they are not looking for an easy way of life. They choose the road with obstacles. I choose the road less traveled, the road with the most obstacles, because that road will teach me how to be great. The results from traveling the same road with everyone has not proven to give good results.

The people who live their lives without sacrifice—the ones who party in their younger days, have women, and pop bottles eventually get to their thirties and have nothing to show for their lives. They're not as established because they didn't sacrifice and instead spent time living in the moment.

We have to plan for our years ahead, plan to make sacrifices to get ourselves a better life in the days ahead. We have to plan to do better. You must have a plan so that you will know at the end of the journey things will get better. Twenty-four hours... twenty-four hours... That's all you have in a day. There is not as much time as people truly believe there is.

2020 should have taught us how fragile and delicate time is. We lost an entire year in 2020—an entire year was stolen from our lives. We were not programmed to sit in our house for the entire year. Twenty-four hours—the year went by so fast. Never have I seen a year go by that fast.
Realize that it does not matter what your circumstances are today, Queue it the pity party and start making sacrifices to change your circumstances as no one is going to feel sorry

for you. They will not care if you are a good person. Your good virtues play no role in making a better life for yourself. The world is very selfish, everyone thinks about themselves.

By teaching our children and by teaching ourselves on how to capitalize on the time we have in the day, we're putting ourselves ahead of the rat race. Running on the same wheel as everyone will not bring about a change in your life, you have to make a decision to change your life. How can you change in order to determine your success? Use this list:

1. Save your money

2. Listen more

3. Change your friends—show me your friends and I'll tell you who you are and who

you'll become.

Be willing to make the sacrifices—while everyone is sleeping, you have to get up. Nothing happens by chance, everything happens with sacrifices—while everyone else is traveling and shopping and acquiring liabilities, you need to save. The person who saves puts themselves in a better position. Capitalize on your day—stop expecting the world to help you—be willing to kick in the door. It's not what you say, it's what you do. Talk is cheap conversation that can be bought. Sacrifice and work hard. Stop wasting your time, as your time is valuable.

Most people sit back and wait for things to change. Time management is an extreme necessity in life, but presents a great struggle to many. In order to manage your time better, you must know what you want to do and when you will do it. When time is managed effectively, one is able to stay consistent, proactive, and execute rather than be reactive and in catch-up mode. Twenty-four hours a day goes by very fast when you are building an empire. Procrastination is a key factor in not being successful. Therefore, we must avoid procrastination by distancing ourselves from all of the potential distractions. A great way to maximize your time is to effectively plan each day from the night before. This will prevent ideas and activities from leaving your mind and it prepares you for an efficient and successful day.

Understanding time is very important. Time is the most valuable asset that anyone can have. Twenty-four hours in a day go by very fast and we must learn to evaluate how we are spending our time. No more sitting around and wasting time because every second, every minute, and every hour matters. We are getting closer to the end. Time is not on our side unless we take advantage of it. Remember, all hours are not created equal. Orienting our work lives around the hours we put in is a way of avoiding the responsibility of using our consciousness and our energy in the best possible way. Execute, execute, execute by guarding your time wisely. Different tasks require different types of hours output. Take time to slow down, pay attention, and notice the world around us, minutes, seconds, hours, slow down. Have you ever thought that there are not enough hours in a day to accomplish everything? Track your time, be proactive, minimize distractions, and value every moment. Your time should be treated as the most valuable commodity you possess. Every day you wake up, repeat to yourself, "Twenty-four hours," over and over. Remind yourself that your time is the most important thing. Value your time and understand what to do with it. Carpe Diem!

Chapter 5
Man-child

When I was a child I spoke as a child, I understood as a child, I thought as a child, I reasoned like a child but when I became a man, I put away my childish things. *I Cor. 13:11*

I've noticed as a man a lot of people aren't holding themselves to a standard of what a man is. Growing up, my definition of a man was based on how many women he could have, how much money he had, how physical he was, and how well he fought. As a man now, I realize most of these factors aren't true.

As an adult I'm seeing this isn't right; something isn't right, this can't be right.

As men, we have to hold ourselves to a better standard. My standard includes integrity, principles, insight, and the willingness to put himself last for his family. This was the conclusion I came to about what a man is. A lot of people factor in how many women they sleep with. However, that does not make you a man. You are not a man. You are a gigolo. Man and gigolo are very different terms, very different definitions.

Many men take money from their children to put into another home. How do you call yourself a man when your home or your children are left without your support and you're not taking care of them? How do you call yourself a man when your woman is out working and out performing you when it comes to the economics of your home? And I'm not going to degrade a man because your woman makes more than you. But if you're not pulling your weight as a man, then there is no way you can be a man.

A lot of people think they're a man because they're tough, or their physicality is outstanding—that does not make you a man. I know some guys who are not physical at all but they hold high standards of integrity and they're very much accountable—that is a man.

When we compare the man child of today, we hear of too many excuses such as my mother did it, my father did it, my father abandoned me, the white man keeping me down, they were oppressors, or the black man has setbacks. The blame has even been put on society for how they behave. Don't get me wrong, I'm not saying the man-child epidemic is only among black men. Man-child is a mindset and it is present in all types of men of varying races, cultures and ethnicities. It spans across all cultures and diversities There are man-children everywhere and that has occurred because a standard has not been held because they blame society for their behavior. Society is what it is, but you have to set the tone in your house. Whatever is wrong or right in society, your children don't have to be subject to that because the standard is set at home. Everything starts at home. Being a father and being a mother starts at home.

Education has to be developed in the household as a standard, meaning it has to be taught in your home. Education should be a standard in your home.

I tell guys all the time, "Using a woman does not make you a man." Some men feel great that they're getting money from a woman, using a woman's car, but that doesn't make you a man, it makes you a bum. Now when that woman disrespects you because she does not see the true traits of a man, you become upset. You shouldn't be upset; she does not see you as a man because you are not holding yourself to the standard of what a man should be. Some women will date these men and tolerate man-children because they want a man to come home to but when they get mad the real repercussions of how they feel come out verbally and they will tell you about how you're not a man. I can't blame a woman for feeling that way but also I can't blame the woman for wanting a man who comes home at night. So, we have women who want to have a man at home but also tolerates that man who is not really a man and has no standards. The woman has to even lower her standards to facilitate a man-child.

As a father of a daughter, I sympathize for this new generation—not the entire generation, but some. The standards have definitely changed over time. A lot of women are taking on the roles of men while men take on the standards of women. Roles can normally interchange at various times. For instance, you can be the breadwinner and then you lose your job, so the woman becomes the breadwinner. I'm not basing economics on who is the man and who is the woman. What I'm saying is that there are a lot more women out there who are tougher than the men. Being tough is defined as the resilience to stay fighting, the resilience to not give up, to provide, to understand that even though I'm a single mother I'm going to keep fighting. That's the new standard for women now because there are many man-children out there.

Men, hold yourself accountable and stop making excuses. Instead of thinking you can beat up other men, go pay bills and support your woman. I thought a man was someone who supported a home, who took care of their family but now it seems as though the men are changing the standard because society is so hard on everyone. Being a man means making sacrifices. No one will feel sorry for you with all your excuses. I grew up without my father and certainly learned instincts a lot later. But I had to learn them quickly and realized that's not the way a man should be. A lot of boys grow up to be a man child because they're being spoiled by mothers. Men become entitled because mothers spoiled them and so they're looking for women to take care of them the way their mother took care of them. So, men aren't looking for a woman, but looking for a mother. Men are proud in the passenger seat of the car of a woman.

I'm certainly not the superman of men, but I'm an alpha and people will know I'm an alpha because of how I conduct myself. It's sad that in 2022, we are living with man-children.

In the last five to seven years, black women have opened up the most businesses in America. I'm fascinated and I'm happy, but that's sad. In the movie *Baby Boy*, Jodie was the man- child who did not want to grow up. His mom tried to live as she raised her son but the son still wanted to be coddled. In that movie we saw the womb and men don't want to leave the womb; they want to stay on the nipple milk of their mother. This is sad. This is the society we're living in where more and more man-children are being born and reared. Toughness is not defined as a man shooting someone or fighting someone—that actually makes you a coward. A true man provides and sacrifices. By no means does toughness make you a man. It's the smallest part of a man, never the focal point.

A man-child continually lives at home depending on parents and never helps to offset bills. Men of today are not impressive, they're not providers, they're not tough, and are very excuse-ridden. They blame everyone for the state of their lives. Blame yourself for the situation you're in, wasting your day, sleeping late—don't blame society for that.

Most people don't realize what a real man is. Many women are carrying men on their backs while the men are relaxing and allowing the women to carry them to a place of success.

Hence women disrespect men as she has settled and tolerated. She'll love you because her heart is with you, but she does not respect you. Intimacy with a woman. manipulation of a woman with your words, does not and will not make you a man. A woman will trust you because she respects you and knows you'll protect her and nurture her. These attributes produce a very different woman. A woman will not submit to a man she does not trust or respect, or does not see that standard of a man. She will sleep with you but not respect you, will love you but not respect you. When we argue with our parents, we reserve our comments because we respect them. Same with a woman. She will reserve her comments when she respects him, when she does not let her mouth go.

A boy is a boy, a man is a man. A man understands that he has to sacrifice to put his family in a better position and understands he must hold himself to that standard.

When I was a child I spoke as a child, I understood as a child, I thought as a child, I reasoned like a child but when I became a man, WHEN I BECAME A MAN, I put away my childish things. I Cor. 13:11

Chapter 6
Sista Sista

I grew up with a single mother, as such, I observed the strengths and values of a single mother. My mom set the standard of how I should view and respect women. As a result, I held women in high regard. Now that I'm an adult, I'm seeing how these standards are changing.

By no means am I saying that men set the standard for women. But we should care about how we view the opposite sex. Society has created the battle of the sexes. From a brother to my sisters, I want you sistas to know that your value is not in your body. Your value is in your mind and what you can contribute to the household of a family.

Mother Earth has a high value on women. What allows me to know this is because the womb that fertilizes and incubates a child is the giver of life. A lot of women don't understand that they set the tone in families and in society. Women have to learn how to block out the noise of society. A lot of the noise has created insecurities and a lot of females are engaging in these insecurities. They are allowing society to tell them that their value is based on their body parts. From a brother to a sister, I'm here to tell you that your value is not just in what your body looks like. Don't be offended by this, but you're worth so much more.

As a man I wonder what's going on with women today. Not the women with integrity and the women who carry themselves as a woman not as a girl. There is a huge difference between a woman and a girl. There has to come a time when everyone decides to make a choice to enter adulthood. SISTA! SISTA!

I'm not impressed by some of the women today. Some of the women conduct themselves as little girls. They are doing nasty things that maybe children would do. I can understand if a guy undresses you with his eyes but these days women leave nothing to behold. If you think I'm not honest about this point, take out your phone and scroll down your timeline.

Some women will say a lot of men try to talk to me, but when many men are trying to talk to a woman it may be attributed to the fact that she appears to be an easy catch. Not all men are coming to you because they genuinely want to be with you. Some women conduct themselves in such a way that men can already see that they're an easy play. The volume of men trying to talk to you is not necessarily because you are beautiful, it's more because you are an easy prey so men are more prone to go after you. SISTA! SISTA!

Coming from a single mother I loved the fact that my mom carried herself a certain way. Certain things she never allowed me to see, certain things I never witnessed. Real women don't allow their children to see certain things.

What has been occurring with women in today's society? Many women are degrading themselves. But here's the catch, if you put yourself out for the village then you wouldn't attract a king. Exposing yourself to the village will not lure a king. You will always lure lower end men from the village.

A king wants a woman who stands for something. The woman who is morally inclined. If you make certain decisions, you will be held to a higher standard. Men sleeping around are viewed as a man. Women will entertain men who sleep with a lot of men because that's just what they do. But here's the catch 22, if the woman sleeps around, no one wants her. Men grade higher, they don't grade as soft as women grade when choosing the opposite sex. Women will choose men who are not really being men and not living up to the standard of a real man. However, men will not do any such thing. They don't want to walk into a room with a woman and know that anyone and everyone has slept with that woman on their arm. When women sleep around, it will cost them; there's a repercussion to that. Your selection is now from the bottom breeders. You wouldn't get a selection from the elite guys because you didn't carry yourself within an elite standard. Women don't like to be judged harshly but you have to remember you eventually want to be married, and when a man is choosing you to be his wife, he is judging very hard. Men are never willing to compromise on their choice for a life mate. Men are hyper sensitive when it comes to choosing their mate. When men see the last man his woman was dating and he's not up to standard, his thoughts are, "Wait, what were you thinking?" Men can't stomach the same things women can. Women can forgive things men can never forget. When women cheat on a man, most men cannot forgive it. In his heart he always thinks on the sexual encounter and it will hinder him and the relationship because he can't see his woman with another man. Women are psychologically stronger than men and can deal with their man being with another woman.

The integrity of women these days is certainly under a spotlight especially since women are now sleeping around and see nothing wrong with it. This lowers your value when dealing with the opposite sex. Most men don't want to date a "Ho." But a man will date a woman who is a "Ho" to him in the bedroom. Most guys want a lady on the street but a freak in the bedroom.

A lot of women now want to settle down at an older age, however, men can't handle your past sexual escapades. Men cannot handle a woman who has slept around.

To a real man, sex appeal is not you dressing half naked. All that does is cause men to be lured to you as an easy kill and that's reality. Wanting to be sexy and looking fire is not always good as the men are only coming to you because of what you look like. Men grade extremely hard and are very selective with their choice of women.

Being with a woman that has cheated is very difficult, the thoughts are always in our minds. Most men can't forgive cheating. Women will stay with cheaters a lot more than men will stay with cheaters.

We must teach our young minds to view themselves differently and view their sexuality with value, with respect.

Men, when looking to sleep with a woman, are not thinking of a commitment or more than one time. On the other hand, women are thinking long term. I myself am very mature when it comes to making that decision to be responsible. We are always thinking of the thrill and after the thrill, we then think. Women think more. But a lot of women are not thinking these days. We see women expressing themselves on social media with twerking and being superficial. Why would a man be attracted to a woman who does just that and has nothing else ascribed to her? Your social media determines how that man will interact with you, will it be just sex based or will it be more beneficial? Your posts can easily indicate you need attention when you're only posting half naked pictures and videos of yourself twerking. In this regard women are begging social media for attention. When social media and its success are your life, you're not thinking of any economic success, your mind is just focused on things that are of no importance and that sends a very powerful message to men.

Remember the analogy of the horse, the donkey and the zebra. When you see them, you don't really know what they are because they all look similar. Now a race starts and the horse takes off, the zebra comes behind him, last comes the donkey who is the slowest and comes last. However, most men chase the donkey, but a donkey is really just an ass. All men see is ass; they're busy chasing ass; they don't ever pay attention to the top breed of these animals which is the Zebra - the thoroughbred - the diva, the classier woman who can get them to the finish line faster. There are the horses of women, the zebra and the donkey, same as with men. A woman has to also find herself a zebra not a donkey. Some people will never get to the finish line because they're running the race with a donkey. Two donkeys will never get much success. A zebra can motivate a donkey. Donkey, horse and zebra are just analogies, not saying people are such. This is where being unequally yoked can have a great impact in one's life. You have to choose carefully. If you are top breed, then you must choose top breed. Your choice must propel you to grow constantly.

A lot of women, especially single mothers, must respect themselves when it comes to how you conduct yourselves. My mother demanded respect and therefore has been threaded like a Queen. In order to be treated like a Queen, you must respect yourself.

Women, keep carrying the torch, keep respecting yourself, keep raising the bar of integrity. Be selective about who enters your temple, your temple should be very exclusive. Every man on the block should not be allowed to enter your temple. This will restrict your choice later and have repercussions. Don't ever think that because men are like that, I should be doing it as well. Men shouldn't be doing it either but men can still get a woman even if he's done that. We must recreate the family structure. Both men and women need each other. Society has lied to us to tell us that women don't need a man. That distorts the family structure as God created, ordained and destined it. God destined that a man find a woman and marry and have a whole family. Proven fact: children in a structured home are more successful. Sistas, go back to valuing and respecting yourselves. If no one else loves you, I love you. SISTA! SISTA!

Chapter 7
Power of the Tongue

The Words you use can affect people who respect you a lot. This is because the tongue has a lot of power. It will either uplift or damage. Words have the distinct ability to hurt. I will share my own encounter with hurtful words. One day I took my girlfriend to visit my dad. Now I have never had a great relationship with my dad because he never raised me. There were always underlying issues. We visited him, my dad showed a great face, and then we left. Two days later my girlfriend and I had an argument and she said, "You would have been a better man if your father raised you." Those words stung so deep that it caused me to second guess myself in that relationship. How could a person who loves me use something vulnerable to me to hurt me?

People use the tongue to hurt people at their most vulnerable moments. When we use words at those weak moments to hurt a person, it says how mature you really are. Words can reign over people for the longest time.

Psychological damage is worse than physical damage because physical damage heals. Psychological wounds can stay ten times longer than physical wounds. The tongue can be used to cause ten times more of a psychological wound that is not necessarily transparent. You never see a psychological wound. Psychological wounds cause damage in every area of our lives, in our decision making, in our relationships, in the way we see the world. The tongue has the ability to cause mental illness.

Physical wounds show mental wounds are hidden based on words and things people have said. Words can hinder our growth. Words can reign over your life for a long time.

My friend once told me his wife said one of the nastiest things to him. She told him that she has not been satisfied by him for years. Those words stayed in his head forever. He lost respect for her, still loved her, but never respected her. Negative words stay in our consciousness but pushes us to not respect anymore.

Love is not equal to respect - two different facets. As he stayed with his wife, he had no respect for her. The words caused him such pain - cause and effect - he pretended as though it was okay. He ended up entertaining other women because they made him feel good. He cheated because he wanted a mental connection, he wanted to feel good. Your mate has to be comfortable to say how they feel without you using words to hurt them.

We give power to the things people say and it hinders our growth. Words used in the wrong way can cause a lot of psychological pain.

The things people have said about me have caused me pain and I allowed what people said about me to affect me in a very negative way because I never thought people who loved me could hurt me. I had to learn to live past what people said about me and not allow their words to affect how I live.

We must possess the ability to control our tongue so that we don't hurt people. The tongue is a very powerful weapon and can cause severe pain. The tongue is mentioned in the Bible. Its effect is compared to being sharper than a knife - words can be sharp coming from the right person. Words -verbs, nouns, sentences can cause pain. Things you say to people who respect you can cause a lot of pain. Men pretend that things said do not affect them. Women tend to say things that are very hurtful in the moment of anger. We need to be conscious of what we say. Words can't be taken back whether they say it or not, it hurts and can't be taken back.

One of my stories occurred when my date looked at me and said she felt she could do better than me. This was said as she was angry. Even after that fight I always felt that she really meant it. For the next two years, I always felt that I was not enough, the words and the wound and the pain, the thought was still there; nothing changed. I thought I was masculine and a man so I wouldn't tell anyone and pretended that those words didn't affect me. But within the next two years the relationship degraded. The power of the tongue destroyed that relationship.

Mental illness is deeper than we know. A lot of people suffer from mental illness. A lot of people suffer from PTSD. A lot of people who have been cheated on have trust issues. If they been hurt, they don't want friends. This keeps you back from good opportunities because you're now living based on what previously transpired in other relationships. Pain - psychological pain - hurts - PTSD - trust - pain causes abnormality - because we're conditioned to behave a certain way in response to a situation.

Mental illness is very deep. Psychology itself is deep. The psychological state of a person is not what you see. The present state of a person can seem to be there in that room but not be mentally in that room. Words can entertain a lot of mental illness. Power of the Tongue. Words can be used to encourage, elevate versus pushing down or belittling. Words are useful when they're used to encourage. When words are used to hurt, they are of no use.

Hurt people hurt people using words. A lot of people continue to bleed from that wound caused by words. Being upset is not a reason to use words to hurt a person. Immature people hurt others with words. The power of the tongue. Utilize your tongue to elevate people to motivate people to encourage people to understand people. Have conversations with people and use your tongue to speak positive things into people's lives. Do not use your tongue to declare negative things about your life. If you keep saying you're broke, you're weak, you will always be broke and weak. Instead use your tongue to tell yourself that you will overcome, you are a leader, that I determine every aspect of my life by speaking with my tongue and my actions. The power of the tongue.

Words can alienate a person causing them to retreat to a "safe" space, not necessarily safe, but more unhealthy. The tongue is the most powerful thing a human has and can be used to cause a lot of damage. Verbal abuse is one of the worst abuses a person can endure. Words can become abusive as they stick in the mind of a person and although the person seems healed, they really are hurting. The tongue has no bones but definitely has the power to break a heart into a million pieces. Given the effect the tongue has, we now have to make the choice to speak life. Speak life into the ones who need to be loved.

Speak truth into life and let's eliminate the lies. We should only use words to ensure purpose of being fulfilled, never using words in arrogance or ignorance. We have the ability to use our tongues to change the world, one word at a time, one person at a time. There are times when we need to seriously consider our words before we express them, think about the effect of your words before uttering them. A good number of people in society today carry hurt as a luggage piece arising from dangerous words spoken. This lends to why people's development becomes stunted. Given the grave damage lethal words can cause, let us all recognize and understand the immense effect words have. The power of life and death lie within the tongue, use it wisely.

Chapter 8
The Wonder Years

Dialogue with Mike from the Neighborhood

Me: Oh, that's my boy mike, Hey Mike, what's going on man?

Mike: Hey what's going on fam?

Me: How you been? feel like I ain't see you in forever.

Mike: I'm still here ain't nothing change, I'm still here, I'm still posting, still living like free committee

Me: The world is bigger than this block right here man, I don't want people to think I'm Hollywood or something.

Mike: Nah man I'm here, you're the one that left, I'm still here, I ain't leave man, I still got the bbs', I still got the fourteen chains on my neck, nothing change the block ain't the same without me, I'm still here, I got to be here

Me: Why do you have to be here

Mike: Cause it's not the same without me, the chicks ain't flowing without me, the money not gonna flow. You remember when we was in the club and the bouncer tried to front and I knocked him out.

Me: Yes but that was ten years ago

Mike: That don't mean nothing I'm still me 42 years old I'm litty

Me: Wow, you don't think it's time to move on

Mike: Nah I have moved on like I moved on as far as I own this corner this is my corner

Me: So the building behind is yours

Mike: Well it might as well be, I done shot some people over it so it might as well be everyone know this is my corner, this is mike's corner - MDollar, my corner, my block

Me: So you go by MDollar now.. didn't you just come home.

Mike: Yeah I just did but Me coming home ain't stopping nothing. But Queueue I gotta bust a move, I love you man I really love you, nice seeing you, get next to me Que you need to get next to me

Yeah cause you know some things never change right, you see me shining, even Ray Charles can see me shining.

Me: Quick before you go.. you ever heard of the wonder years

Mike: Yeah you mean the show?

Me: No, the wonder years, that's when people are stuck and they can't move on. You don't think you're stuck in a moment?

Mike: Nah nah nah i been stuck here talking to you but I gotta go get this job but yo nice talking to you, I love you

Both: Be safe bro.

A lot of people are stuck on memory lane, that is enjoyable moments that should have been outgrown but now they're stuck. People still brag about what they did when they were kids, high school etc. and when they were kids.

Recreate new moments, no need to stay on memory lane. Stuck on memory lane because they felt significant, special or popular, there in that period of time. I remember someone reminding me that they were voted most popular in high school. That's irrelevant right now. Would people vote for you as most popular now if they were to see your life and your successes or the lack thereof?

A lot of people have not changed their addresses on memory lane. Whatever they've done before, they hold onto it still there because they felt special and still feel special there. No one cares about what you used to do; they want to know what you are currently doing. Not what you used to do. So many people are stuck on significant moments - glory days - wonder years.

Your wonder years are the years you don't want to move on from. The 40-year-old woman who behaves like she's 13 years old because she's stuck on those moments and can't move on. The wonder years are years that make you feel significant and special.

Personal story - I saw a man from the neighborhood I used to be from. I went to embrace him but he greeted me with "you're Hollywood you don't come around her anymore". He seemed upset that I was doing well. He went on to comment that he sees me on social media flexing. No flexing, social media just shows me living. He accused me of forgetting where I came from. He didn't realize where I came from, that made me who I am today. It was never a contractual agreement that I had to stay where I was. I thought the whole idea was to move on, to do better, to make a better life for my family.

I'm not stuck on those old glory days. I've moved on because I know who I am and what I've accomplished. This man was stuck in those wonder years. My wonder years have become me enjoying my family enjoying my life. It's sad, that because you've moved on with your life, you're seen as a bougie or you're accused of being better than others. A person is not better, they've just made the choice to move on, that does not make them better than anyone. They just don't want to be stuck there. Being confined to a bad neighborhood is not a life sentence. Staying in a bad neighborhood is not your fate. You just need to work extremely hard to get out. Change your mindset and you can get out of there. It's a choice to leave that neighborhood and do better. You have to sacrifice and do what it takes to get out. You don't stay because your momma grew up there. Be willing to work hard to get out.

He said to me; I forgot where I came from. I've learned how to be a man later in life because I was very, very ignorant. My ignorance stemmed from the environment I grew up in. The people's behaviors around me fueled my ignorance. If forgetting where I came from helps me to be a better father, to be economically more stable, so be it. If forgetting where I came from can cause my mother to say "I regret you" to saying "I'm proud of the man you have become," then so be it. I forgot where I came from.

This man could not understand my successes. All he could see was the four-block radius. He didn't realize the world was bigger than what he could see. He further didn't understand the need for a passport when asked. He didn't see the need to travel and experience other cultures. He saw it as a sell out and felt like he needed "to hold the hood down". How do you stand on the corner all day and not own anything there? But maybe that gives people a feeling of entitlement and comfort.

Life is about evolving, not staying at the same level, but evolving requires change, like forgetting where you came from. This is not disowning the area, this is owning the experiences from which you came. But you should use these experiences to be able to move on and gain successes. A better you allow your family to benefit from the sacrifices you make.

The hood mentality isn't cute. It's your perception that stinks and it controls your results. Your results are controlled by your thinking. Change your mind, change your perception. Change your ideology and you'll have great results. It's a shame when you encounter someone you haven't seen in ten years and their way of thinking and speaking is the same as it was ten years ago. There is no improvement. No evolution. They're stuck in the wonder years - the years they consider to be great - not realizing you must move on and build greater memories. I used to be…but your family suffers as life is not concerned about who you used to be. Your popularity in high school pales in comparison to you standing on the corner begging for money.

Talking about and remembering what you did is not important. They need to realize that your sacrifices and who you want to become start with a mindset which will either make you or break you. Remembering the old is not what I want to do. I don't want to remember my negatives and where and what I used to be because I want to move on to greater things.

The wonder years - some moments come for a time; you have to be comfortable to know it was *just* a moment. Don't get stuck in a moment of time. Bragging on things you did in a childhood when you didn't know better disallows you from moving on as you become so stuck. What never changed is a result of you failing to launch, failing to jump so you're still there.

You cannot change one's mindset if they're not willing to change themselves. Move on from the wonder years, create new moments, understand those moments were just moments in time. God has a greater purpose for you if you'd just let go of the glory days and move on from the wonder years.

Most people find themselves stuck in the moment of their past, constantly dwelling on their wonder years. The past has to be the past, it has to stay in the past. We have to be willing to walk away from our past. We do understand that the past has a role to play in who we are today, but the present is what continues to foster the person you will be. The wonder years prevent us from becoming our best selves. They keep us stuck to a moment that has been gone for many years. It is time to move past and give ourselves the permission to become something great. Those past moments served their purpose in the past, now it's time to focus on what is ahead of you and how to create even greater moments.

Chapter 9
Smoke and Mirrors

BLOCK OUT THE NOISE!! BLOCK OUT THE NOISE!!

Smoke and mirrors are defined as something that is not, something that is true when it's false. Smoke and mirrors give us a false reality. The world is filled with perceptions - some false perceptions.

Some pretend that they're doing better than what you're actually doing - social media is utilized to present a false reality. Social media lets people think we're more established than we are. True definition of Smoke and Mirrors.

A lot of people believe everything they see as long as it's on social media. People are just trying to mimic what they see on social media not realizing that they're only putting themselves further back in the race. A person looks established on social media, so you employ all their mechanics for looking the way they do, including expensive clothes and jewelry. These items however could be fake - smoke and mirrors.

An impression is given to the world that you're doing much better than you really are
Because of perceptions people think what they see is the truth but it isn't. Perception is defined as the ability to see, hear or become aware of something through the senses - the process of becoming something through the senses.

What I believe to be true in my mind can be technically true because I wholeheartedly believe it. People's perception can be whatever they want it to be. A lot of celebrities have used these platforms to make people think they're living better than they really are, they may live better than you but that person can still live paycheck to paycheck just as you. But the perception is they're more established because they present a certain image of being established. BLOCK OUT THE NOISE!

These are people who prefer to have certain designer items and live in an apartment building rather than use that designer money to own a home.

I've noticed men who use these spaces to pretend to be more than what they are so that they can capture prey because women are looking for men who seem to be doing well. For the sake of a certain image - we put ourselves in debt so that we can seem a certain way to resemble an image we see on social media - little do we know what we see on social media isn't always what's true - smoke and mirrors.

Pictures can say a thousand words. Mastering the art of illusion. Illude the mind to be doing something it isn't. Trick of the mind. These things we see on social media are illusions. Showing a liability more than an asset is seen every day. Showing a bank card versus cash. People think

I'm better off with cash to my ear than my card. But my card can have 7 million dollars attached to it and I'm only holding $10,000. It's a perception. Perception - master the art of perception and what you believe to be real. Social media isn't what it really is - it is a smoke and mirrors.

Most of the people selling you get rich ploys are lying and selling you to subscribe to their programs and making you believe that if you buy their program, you will make money fast and easy. Anything given to you from that facet is either wrong or not true.

Smoke and mirrors - people pretend to be a lot more than what they really are. Difference is people believe that if I pretend to be successful therefore, I will manifest success by thinking of success but leave out the work. People believe if you just believe you'll be successful without work; It will not work, you must work.

Everything can't be instant gratification - instagram - everything must be fast. No one gets rich overnight. Social media has captivated so many minds and has used this platform to make people think things are but they're not. For instance, yesterday I was walking and today I'm driving a Ferrari. Not possible. This is why people are believing lies. You will not know that they could have rented the Ferrari. People will show you a live video of vacation but not a live video in their home and that's because of perception. If I can allude you to believing something, I will. If I can get you to believe my lie I will.

If people will use the same energy in pretending to be successful, they can become successful. Use the same energy to act rich to be rich. Most people waste their time pretending - smoke and mirrors.

I look at people as half empty glasses, just because you drive a fancy car does not mean you're established, just because you wear fancy clothes does not mean you're established.

When you'll be successful, you have to weed out the pretenders. Pretenders use platforms to hold the community back to disconnect and bring out non-beliefs in a lot of people.

Sports analogy - football field - I'm the Quarterback and you're the receiver - your job is to catch the ball and run to the end zone. I'm going to throw the ball and you'll catch it. We're 40 yards from touchdown, so you run to the 30, then to the 20 then to the 10 to the 5 to the 4 to the 3 to the 2 you get to the 1 and drop the ball before you get to the end zone. But yet you walk into the end zone and you start celebrating. Did you really score a touchdown? Answer is No. This is what people do when they start celebrating prematurely when they could have scored a touchdown. They're acting like they're more established than they really are and becoming rich to give a good impression so they're working against themselves. You could have scored the touchdown, there were no defenders, but you did not score because you celebrated prematurely. Technically you could have scored if you would have gone all the way to the end zone instead of stopping at the 1 to celebrate. People are celebrating too soon; they're not in the end zone and they haven't scored yet.

If you're not conscious of your financial behaviors, your mental behaviors, your circle of people you're around, you'll never see what you're doing with your resources because you're around people doing the same things with their resources. Everyone doing the same thing is insanity and is stopping you from getting where you should be. What should enable you is preventing you from moving forward; it is a blockade. It is a mental blockade and a mental blockade is harder than a physical blockade. I can climb over a physical blockade but a mental blockade alters you from getting to any level because the mental aspect presents more difficulty. A wise man (Les Brown) once said, "Making a million dollars is easy but believing you can make a million dollars is hard." I believe that to be true. A lot of people have financial skills and can get to a level. What you do with your money determines where you'll go in life. You have to utilize your money to advance you. Stay away from smoke and mirrors - stop pretending. A person must be comfortable with themselves as their success is not determined by what they drive or wear. People are so captivated by what the world believes about them. Stop worrying about what people think. If you lay a brick every day, you'll have a wall eventually but if you never lay one brick, you'll never have a wall. Lay your life's goals, purposes and accomplishments. Don't chase what people think about you. Get in contact with your own reality. People have lost touch with their reality. Social media lies and blurs reality so everyone is busy believing a lie. Social media allows people to lie. So, the mind starts believing the lie, the craziness of the mind. As you tell your mind something, the mind believes it. Some believe their own madness, they believe they're rich. As you speak a lie from the mouth the ear brings that lie in and it eventually alters the mind. People prefer to hear a lie rather than the truth. If you keep repeating the lie, the mind believes the lie. Smoke and mirrors.

Your success and your life trajectory is dependent on what you feed your mind and what you're building. If you're not planting seeds, you will not eat from your garden. You have to plant the seeds and nurture the plants to eat. You will never eat if you don't plant seeds. Life does not happen overnight; it happens from sacrifices, from determination, from knowing how to weed out the smoke and mirrors. Life happens by being conscious of your resources and knowing your economic positioning.

The saddest thing about smoke and mirrors is, we believe these are the people we want to be like but in reality, we're most likely living better than they are. Successful people do not waste time on liabilities or trying to impress others. Some of the influencers we so admire, were we to see them in person, it would break our hearts and leave us in a state of shock.

Some of the alleged "influencers" - the people highly connected to social media - in real life can be heartbreaking. But while it is heartbreaking, it brings you face to face with reality. There are a lot of people who subscribe to the idea of "fake it till you make it." Understanding you have to live about that type of influence. These influences create a narrative of how society should be and that narrative is not always the reality.

Smoke and mirrors is the art of the illusion. People have mastered this art and it has become a hindrance to our culture. We are living in a fake reality. Faking it will never progress a person or bring them to a place of opportunities or success. It keeps them in a place of poverty and living through a "smoking mirror." In order to get a job, you must present experience on your resume. Smoke and mirrors does not provide any experience, instead it embraces false perceptions. In order to be successful and gain meaningful experience one must work and work hard. Pretending to be confident, happy or successful for the people in the insta world to be impressed by your fake lifestyle will only present you with failures. Success demands that we focus, we work and we work hard. Smoke and mirrors - False Reality never brings success.

BLOCK THE NOISE!!

Clean the smoke and mirrors so you can see the reality.

Chapter 10
If the Walls could Speak

As a young man, I wanted to prove I was a man and ended up in circumstances that I'd never want to be in again. In an attempt to prove my masculinity, I ended up incarcerated. While in incarceration, I saw and had to learn who I was. Behind those walls there was no noise but me and my voice, I heard my voice because there was no noise. No noise allowed me to hear myself.

The walls spoke to me. They told me I have to grow up a lot. I heard the voice of so many people saying what would happen to me if I didn't listen. The walls spoke to me.

Department of corrections does not correct anything. I had to correct myself. I had to tell myself the truth, there were no more distractions, no more outside noise, no more partying, no more chasing girls, no more selling drugs, just me paying back my restitution as consequences for what I have done. The walls spoke to me and those Walls spoke loudly.

I heard Testimony of others. They can't be forgotten because they made me cry. Some of the things I've seen I can't forget, it's impossible to forget. Impossible to forget grown men crying because they miss their family, impossible to forget <u>children</u> sentenced to life.

Department of correction did not correct but permitted more Mental illness than anything.
There are a lot of children being overcharged with long stints, being removed from their families for long periods of time.

While in jail I met a 19-year-old boy who got incarcerated on his 18th birthday. I was speaking with him after his trial was complete. He told me he was sentenced to 40 years. I tried to explain he would be here for 35 years minimum and about when he gets home and which woman he'll be with. He couldn't understand that he had a long time to go, a long time to hear the walls speak.

The walls speak in jail - if you can hear the cries of the wall, it makes you very, very sad.

A lot of people get the lost and found syndrome, loss until it's time to come home, then you're found. Issue is, most people go away and come back the same age because they lack experience. A person at 19 years old comes home at 30 years old. They're still 19 years old mentally with no experience other than the jail experience. Nothing else has enabled him to grow beside the jail experience. Most people wear the jail experience as a badge of honor because they have no other experiences.

The walls talk. And me being behind these walls, I couldn't believe I was there. Every criminal thinks they're the smartest criminal. I never thought I'd end up in prison, never I'm too slick, I can beat the system, I know what I'm doing. Most people understand the money aspect or fun aspect of their illegal activity but never learn the consequences. Losing my freedom was the hardest thing I ever experienced in my life. This 19-year-old who could not understand that he'll be in there for a long time hurt. I wanted to tell him, "Use this time to educate your mind because you'll be here for a very long time." He's about to lose his youth as he started this path of imprisonment as a boy but will return home as a man. The walls talk.

If you've ever been in a closet, imagine being locked in there for 23 out of the 24 hours. 23 and 1 - you're locked in a closet for 23 hours and 1 hour you're out. The expectation that a person comes home from that experience being rehabilitated is false. Inmates experience death and torment in that space. Not everyone in prison is guilty; some are innocent in there. Some didn't have the resources to be equipped to be found innocent.

Many nights I stared at the four walls, they spoke to me, they made me value my freedom. I had tons of truthful conversations with myself. We need to have more conversations with ourselves. As I did my time, I decided to never be in this situation ever again. The system is designed to fail us as it's a business. This country I love, the USA, will use people's life as a business. Mental illness is so prevalent in prison. This environment makes you so aggressive.

My new bunk mate walks in and I told him I don't sleep on top bunks. He said, "Listen youngster, I'm older and I am not doing the top bunk." I responded with I don't care you're getting on the top bunk. He eventually convinced me to get on the top bunk. We talked all night. The next morning, he said, "Youngster, what are you doing this morning"? I said I'm gonna stay in the cell, he said come with me to the eating hall. We sat down and ate breakfast, but I couldn't help seeing all the eyes staring at me which I couldn't understand. He convinced me to go to the rec yard. As we got there, he clapped his hands three times. He said, 'Youngster I'm MU Jah E and if I didn't get the top bunk this morning, you would have been dead." This was the first time in my life I felt so vulnerable that I could have been hurt. As a young man I felt I could never be hurt, I was superman, you couldn't tell me anything. I could fight anyone. But here I was so vulnerable and couldn't do anything. As he clapped his hand 30 Muslim inmates lined up. He then said he was the IMAN of the prison. He ran the prison when it came to the Muslims. That experience was a wake-up call because I never thought I could be hurt. I thought I was indestructible. He taught me, talked with me as a peer. For the very first time, a man took the time to spend with me, to teach me, to input into my life, in an attempt to ensure that I never came back to this place. He made me feel comfortable. He taught me that men can be vulnerable at times; he taught me that men have feelings. However, society tells us that men should be strong and not feel and be this masculine being. More men, if they expressed themselves more will have fewer issues. So many men are still trying to prove their masculinity. You're not weak because you feel or fail; you're human.

The walls talked and they spoke to me. I heard so many different testimonies of guys being here for 10 years, or 20 years. Guys have been there so long they don't know what an iPhone is. They have no concept of wireless computers; they're accustomed to buffering. No idea of what an iPad is. Stocks and bonds are an unknown language. They have lost their sense of reality.

Walls talk. Walls make inmates feel conflicted - as they don't want to be on the outside - they end up going back because it's okay to be there. They're in a space where they don't want to leave.

Those walls helped me to become a man and hold myself accountable. Being in prison was not good or fun. I had to grow up. It was like teaching a child to ride a bike, taking off the training wheels and pushing you to ride. I heard myself, I read and I talked to myself. I read so much I felt uncomfortable if I didn't read. Reading is necessary as nuggets are hidden in books. Prison got me to read and learn. Reading freed up my mind, even though I was confined to a space, I was free. I was in that space but not in that space because my mind was free. I realized I was stronger than this place, because this place did not make me. I was there but my mind wasn't there. I was in jail physically but my mind wasn't there, reading allowed my mind to leave that prison. Reading took me to different places all over the world. Reading allowed me to see how powerful my mind really was.

Prison showed me that everything in life starts with a thought, followed by an action, backed by a plan that is either negative or positive. Sometimes in life we look at our current state and we allow ourselves to stay at this level because of fear of the unknown. My incarceration allowed me to face the realization that growth begins with me, the person. Growth is a personal mission that one must embark on alone. Being alone gave me the tools to self-meditate on my past pains, and my past mistakes but it also proved that I needed to enhance my vocabulary. One of the words I had to embrace was accountability. There was never a time in my life where I took responsibility for my actions; a time where I actually listened to myself; a time where I expected everyone to feel sorry for me. The walls spoke to me and at first, I tried to ignore them. The more I tried to ignore them, the louder the voices got. The voices got so loud that I actually thought I was going crazy. I was waking up at nights in my cell in cold sweats, yelling at the top of my lungs for the voices to leave me alone. I was tormented by my past and disturbed by the voices. The voices had very strong and destructive messages. These messages reminded me that I was now a criminal, that I would be nothing, that I'd never accomplish anything in life. One of my sleepless nights was the night before my birthday. As the clock said 12 am and my birthday came in, I made the decision at that moment to face the noise, be a man and face my reality. Excuses were my escape from my reality. Listening to the voices allowed me to start making hard, but necessary changes; changing my perspective - changing my responsibility as to the way I had lived my life up to this point. Accountability became the evidence of need because of the need for healing. Deep rooted wounds needed psychological bandages. I decided to embrace the greatest healing that would ever take place, but first I had to have a conversation with myself and face the truth. My renewed mind blocked all access to the lies I previously lived. The walls spoke and I spoke back. At that point I received closure to the hurt pangs and the pains I had hidden with

99

lies. With closure came peace. The walls provided truth, light, understanding and peace and with these attributes I encountered a new me.

The walls talked. As they talked, I blocked out the noise. You have to know how to block out the noise even in that environment. In my darkest moments of prisons and those walls, I was able to navigate my mind out those walls. You control your mind no matter where you find yourself. In my cell, in this small little closet, I talked to myself, I questioned myself as to all the excuses I've used, why did I blame the world for my actions. As I addressed these issues, I started to grow and started to learn who I was. Those speaking walls could never imprison a powerful mind. As I exited my time of incarceration, my mind met my body and became free because I learned how to navigate those speaking walls.

Chapter 11
Bridging the Gap

I'm learning that a relationship between elderly and younger is beneficial as it enables both to learn a skill. Young people will learn not to make the same mistakes and both will increase knowledge as to the community as a whole.

There is an extreme disconnect between younger and older. It seems like no respect exists between these two groups. The younger people don't respect older people and older people don't respect the younger. Therefore, there is a breakdown in communication. Neither one understands each other.

The next reason for the disconnect is that the older people forget when they were younger. It seems like the generational morals and principles and integrity and parenting have changed. These parenting changes have created the children that the older complain about.

So, of course there is a disconnect because the way the last generation parented from how this generation is parenting.

There is a lot more entitlement, a lot more people feel entitled. So now we have a generational gap from the ones that worked extremely hard to allow this generation to enjoy the fruits of their labor but here's the catch: they want the fruit but not the labor. So, there is the gap and that's a big gap. Gap between the hard workers gives this generation the opportunity to enjoy the fruits of their labor but young people don't want to work for the fruits.

We must blame parents for how and what they teach their children, work ethic is taught. Sacrificing and grinding and working hard and wanting more are taught. We can't expect a 21-year-old to wake up and want to conquer the world but never had the experience doing it.

The older generation work extremely hard not to understand the youth. You can't connect with them if you don't understand them. Take yourself back in time and see they're making the same mistakes you made. We pray and put them in environments where they're growing up. Connection is necessary for understanding.

We also have a lot of parents living through children. Now we have a child who is being ostracized or yelled at or always challenged because you (the parent) made certain decisions you don't want your child making. But for children to grow up, they have to make mistakes and learn. Don't be your child's friend. Understand their age and be understanding of their development into an adult.

When assessing, comparing and contrasting the older and the younger age groups, we can use this analogy - Lebron James and Michael Jordan - the older generation will see Michael Jordan as the greatest player but the younger generation will see Lebron as the greatest player. They are both great players but specific to each generation. For the younger generation, it may be harder but it is our job to make it easier for the next generation.

Children are taught respect, so if I meet a child and he has no respect, it means it was never taught. Should I be mad at the child or at the parent who never taught respect? Bridging the gap, we have to find a level ground. It seems like we're losing the younger generation. But we must connect to them by understanding versus judging.

We were taught to honor our parents and respect our neighbor. In addition, to treat others how we want to be treated. These were the general rules of the land.

In today's world, we're seeing the difference between generations when we observe flip phones versus iPhones. Our world is now technology driven.

One thing we must realize is that we cannot force our generational belief on our children. Their music is so different - we should take the time to understand why they like this music. What about this music is so enticing to them?

Times are changing, we cannot afford to become obsolete. However, certain things of the past must stay relevant; things such as - morals, beliefs, willingness to sacrifice, integrity. These things were all seen in the older generation. Therefore, we must close the gaps between generations with understanding and not judgment. In this age, we have now found ourselves living in, the younger generation have allowed their opinions and feelings to be the driving force behind many of their decisions. Experience has taken a back seat to the feelings and opinions of the youth. Please understand, before you can age you must begin at one. The experience brings wisdom and knowledge. It would allow us to think that the older generation is not capable of understanding the younger generation. Today, there is no value placed on knowledge and experience. The gap between generations derives from the lack of experience, knowledge and wisdom. A lot of mistakes made today would not be made if the younger generation took the time to just listen. Listen to experience, let it be your guide.

Chapter 12
Day 2

What is change - it is to make someone or something different - alter or modify, replace something with something else, substitute one thing for another - newer and better.

Day 2 occurs when that change takes place in you. When you're no longer who you used to be even though you were that person for a long time. When the old you is substituted by the new you, and you have become modified. When day 2 occurs, you have to change the people you're around.

Some people think you should stay around your day 1 people, but the problem with the people of day 1 is that they can't see who you are on Day 2. Be willing to leave people behind and move on. Day 1 can only see who you were, day 2 people see you for who you are now.

You're no longer that day 1 person. Day 2 is a person that you're trying to become now - in order to express greatness and walk on purpose, you have to be willing and comfortable to walk away from who you were (day 1) - those moments when you were. Be comfortable to embrace new people as they represent your day 2.

New people bring out the greatness in us. Staying loyal to failure - to mediocrity - will not permit you to become a better you. Staying loyal to a lesser you, will only bring you to failure; you will never become who you were destined to be.

Day 1 accepts you for who you are - but not becoming who you should be because you're not being provoked to be better. In order to be great, you have to be willing to be uncomfortable. Uncomfortable feelings allow you to grow. Diamonds go through a vigorous process to become a diamond. Being uncomfortable gives you different exposures, different mindsets. A different mindset will change your trajectory.

The people you're around either prevent you from growing or propel you to grow. Be conscious of the people you're around. I used to think having five or ten thousand dollars was a lot because I was around people who didn't have a lot of money themselves. Therefore, I was not inspired to have more money. My competition was not that great -I really wasn't doing that well but in my mind I was. As day 2 becomes greater, I must surround myself with people who are greater than I was. If you are smarter than the people you're in a circle with, chances are your circle isn't that good. Your circle should be of a certain level, of people who motivate you to do more. In that day 1 circle, you breathe complacency, you breathe contentment, you become stagnated because you're not around people who are propelling you to be greater. Be around people who make you feel uncomfortable as that propels you to change ways about yourself. When the days change, you'll see the change in yourself. In order to become greater on day 2, you have to want to change yourself. In order to see these changes, one has to make sacrifices and changes to their environment. People, places and things, people determine your mindset, the places you go determine your outlook on life and the things you do tell me who you really are.

People want such great things for their lives but they're not sacrificing or putting themselves around people who are holding them accountable. Why would I want people to accept me as broke? Why not be around people who say it's not good enough, you can do better.

Do all you can to the best of your ability, so it's ingrained in your natural character. Be great no matter where you find yourself; it becomes a part of who you are.

You don't have to stay around your day 1s. On day two I'm trying to become better. When I'm stuck on day 1s,

I can't see the change in me. I have to alter my mind to day 2 so I change the trajectory of my life. I see that I need to be around people who make my life easier in order to get me to where I want to be. I need to be around people who make me better, not around people who tell me what I want to hear. If you feel you're successful, you will not work hard to become successful; but if you're told you're not, you'll work hard to be successful.

People who knew who you were don't want to see. you grow. Big ideas delivered to a small- minded person will automatically knock your idea down because they can't see themselves growing further than where they're presently at. Motivated people hearing your idea will push you to do better. The day 2 people will motivate and say, "Let's push and move." They are not complacent; they will challenge you. Day 1 will allow you to stay complacent because if you move on, they will fear losing you. Misery loves company.

Someone cannot want you to be great and motivate you when they can't be great and they're not motivated themselves. Becoming great is not just spoken, it is hard work. Be around people who will make your life easier so that you can become great. I can't want to be more like God if I hang around people who are not of God and are doing bad things; that's a conflict. I can't be an athlete and hang out with guys who don't want to train. I can't get good grades hanging out with people who don't work for great grades. This is a contradiction. Most people are who they associate themselves with. We cannot be around people and go places and do things that don't lend to us being great – that is a contradiction.

Being comfortable will never allow you to fulfill your purpose and be great. People have died being comfortable and never reached their maximum potential. Become uncomfortable - get new friends - get out of the comfortable circle - go after the day 2s and leave the day 1s behind.

In order to be successful, one must embrace new opportunities, new environments – and be uncomfortable. When you are challenged, you will see that things become achievable when actions are applied. Day ones tend to be a major reason most people cannot change. Embracing a person who does not want to change becomes extremely difficult. Day ones will constantly declare that progress is not possible, that success cannot happen. On the other hand, Day twos see things from a completely different perspective. It is much easier for you to grow with Day twos because as you grow, they will grow. As your goals change, so do their goals; they will plan for their future. They view self-improvement as highly necessary and as a key element of growth. They will never permit you to stay at the same place for the rest of your life. In order to change, one must become uncomfortable. An old dog cannot and will not learn new tricks and why is this? Because the dog is surrounded by other dogs who aren't learning nor teaching new tricks. Humans are naturally creatures of habits and habits you have learned are habits that have ultimately led you to your current position. Habits create an environment that one develops over time. In order to create new habits, one must move on to a new environment and new people. This is the total value of the Day two individuals. They allow a new energy to enter your life, an energy that will create new motivation, new beliefs thereby allowing for new goals. Day twos provide a new outlook, a new vision. When Day twos are around, you see yourself in a light you've never seen yourself in before. A lot of people have embraced the sandbox theory where they continue to stay in the same sandbox because they grew up with those people in that same sandbox. They feel a sense of nostalgia and sentiment, so they refuse to grow past the sand box.

Chapter 13
Unity - You and I

They say teamwork makes the dream work. Unity is defined as a condition of harmony - Equality or state of being made as one-you and I. Most relationships do not have team work - man will work to do his agenda and the woman works on her agenda. Family structure is actually being diminished more and more every day.

People don't care about the longevity anymore - instead we value a quick fix more.

No more unity - no more two sacrificed as one and working as a unit. No one should look to see who makes more money. That's irrelevant, it's ours, we're a team. Sometimes most relationships are based on who does more based on economics - who do more - shouldn't be like that. I am sacrificing for you and you for me so ultimately, we get to the goal. Stop looking at each other for what you can do for me but what we can do for each other.

Economics is not dependent on who does more, but all together getting to one goal.

What can we do together? What is your value? Are we helping each other to get to their destination?

Why would you want people in your life to help you but you don't help others? That makes no sense. There is no more investing. A relationship is an investment. This investment should be that we build each other up. We help each other and we take care of each other.

These perspectives have been tossed out. There is now a new agenda. Economics have controlled relationships so much to the magnitude of people valuing money more than the actual relationship. Money should never measure success or how accomplished our relationship is.

Two successful people can come together and be miserable because money isn't everything. Just because they're two successful people doesn't mean they're compatible. Compatibility has dwindled down so much that people don't care about who they're dating as long as they bring home the bacon. That's very sad.

A woman and a man should not be measured by what they can do for each other but for what they can do together. Can they help each other? Can one mold the other? Relationships should be about challenges and making for greater selves. There is a state of emergency, no more unity, no more you and I. I did this….me, me, me… I did this, I did that, I paid for this, I paid for that - no more teamwork. A championship is only won by different people playing different roles in different facets and accomplishing the goal. Minds come together as a unit. "I'm gonna do what I got to do" has no place in a relationship; that's applicable in a situationship. Unity is to make each other's lives easier.

It takes a specific mindset to be on a team and an understanding that harmony is everything.

Society has devalued relationships. The numbers on marriages are failing and falling. There is no more you and I, only me and I - traded the US for me. Many are looking for relationships but know they're not willing to work and be a team. We are to build each other up so therein should be our issues in the home. Sacrifice the "me" for the greater "we." Change the perspective so that there is more unity. Many people have chosen to not understand the factor of unity. This has happened because our society is selfish; we are only seeing selfishness.

The goal should be to motivate each other and stand as a unit. Relationships are about sacrificing and compromising and that's the reality of unity. A dream with a date becomes a goal. A goal made by the steps together becomes a plan. A plan backed and followed by the actions of togetherness becomes your reality. Unity allows us to achieve greater goals as we're doing it together, better two than one. Marriage provides a safe place for individuals to grow together, to develop together and to put away selfishness. Several socioeconomic factors such as income, education, marriage rate declining and race have contributed to the broad decline in home ownership.

The mentality of competition has destroyed many of our relationships and marriages. Instead of working as a team, men and women become competitive. They do not work together but work against each other. There is no building together and achieving together. Instead, there is jealousy and envy and eventually here comes selfishness, thereby eliminating the team. This competition between men and women has created wars and it is very evident that men versus women and the battle of the sexes is destroying society. Competition breeds separation.

There is no me, or I, only us. Unity - harmony - you and I working together for a greater good.

Chapter 14
4th Quarter

1st Quarter

In the first Quarter of a life, the child is born defenseless and senseless. No care in the world - no feelings - no understanding. This is the fetus stage. In this stage we have no choice who we are born to or the neighborhoods we're born into. At this stage we couldn't care less. We have no understanding of anything. The first Quarter is careless, a baby has no responsibilities. All you know is the bosom of your mother nurturing your body and changing you and feeding you. There are no responsibilities, there is no thinking. There is only a free mind.

Development in the first Quarter is taught by only exposure as performed by parents. There is no wrong or right. The only wrong and right are taught by parents. All we know is we need food, we need diaper change and when we're ready to sleep. As a baby we know no responsibilities, we don't know what neighborhoods we were born into or the street we live on. Everything we need in this Quarter is just simply given to us. This Quarter presents as the most pliable moments of a child's development. An extreme level of innocence is very visible.

The first Quarter covers the period of birth to 12 years old. A lot of issues that surface in your later days are made or based on things that happen in this first Quarter. The vital key elements of your development are integrity and principles. Principles learnt as a child cannot be taught as an adult. The curiosity of a child propels that child to touch everything. Their innocence makes them want to see and touch everything. This Quarter in turn prepares you for the 2nd Quarter. This Quarter is preparation for the teenage years. This Quarter a child learns respect, manners and integrity. These principles must be taught in the first Quarter. They must learn how to speak to people and how to carry themselves in the street. These are vital to the development of the young mind. This Quarter creates the later adults we'll see. In this Quarter we believe we can obtain or attain any goal, nothing is impossible. We believe everything is given to us. In this Quarter the parents must teach principles and attributes so that you learn how to transition into the second Quarter.

2nd Quarter

This Quarter covers the teenage into adult years. The rush to grow up is evident in this Quarter. The reason being is that you start noticing responsibilities start changing and you start seeing the things of the world. Things become more transparent, as you start going to school you see different things and have a deeper understanding. Lots of time the first sexual encounter takes place in this Quarter and this makes you think you're an adult. When I was thirteen, I was always wishing I was an adult. Not realizing I was rushing to bills and responsibilities. Boy, if I can go back to thirteen now! But we never think like that when we're thirteen. We only think about getting our own place and driving a nice car. We never realize that it takes massive responsibilities to maintain these things. Second Quarter. In this mindset a lot of adults think they're entitled to things. Entitlement creeps in an extremely heavy manner in this Quarter. We live in a very entitled society. For some, the responsibilities presented push you to develop quickly and to grow into the mindset of an adult. You're seen as a child if you cannot adhere to the responsibilities of an adult. An adult carries a household, carries economic responsibilities that will sustain a home. A child cannot do these things; therefore, a child cannot be an adult if they're not carrying a home. A young adult cannot be the king of a castle as there cannot be two kings in that castle. There can only be one king and that one king is the person who is responsible enough to carry that home. The king of my castle is me, not my child. A lot of children think they're grown because they can drink alcohol and drive a car. Still, you're not an adult.

Children start combatting the teachings of the parents as they start thinking they can do it better and they know more. However, there exists a lack of experience and a lack of knowledge. This Quarter prepared me to be the adult I am today. In my second Quarter days, I thought nothing else matters and nobody can do anything to me, I was untouchable. In my second Quarter days, I thought only what I felt mattered and nothing else. At that young age a lot of people feel like that but this can be attributed to lack of knowledge and lack of experience. Experience teaches you how to be, what to be and what to do and not to do. Experience is the best teacher. A lot of people have to touch the stove to see if it's hot throughout the second Quarter. When they touch the stove and realize its hot, yet still keep touching the stove because they're thinking it can't happen to them. In the second Quarter, we tend to think it's not me, it's not going to be me, I'm exempt; Watch, I'm going to figure it out better and faster than everyone else. What they're really doing is trying to beat a system and navigate through it, but there is no cheat code, no shortcut. It is a process and you have to trust your process. If I navigate this second Quarter well, then my third Quarter can be grand, but I have to properly and effectively navigate through the second Quarter. The Second Quarter prepares you for the third Quarter.

3rd Quarter

In this Quarter the young adult becomes a full-fledged adult. In this Quarter, it's a combination of first and second Quarter. If you're not prepared effectively in the first and second Quarter, you will have issues transitioning to the third Quarter.

Now in the third Quarter, if not prepared, you tend to not want to grow up. The First Quarter prepared you as a child for the responsibilities of the second Quarter. The second Quarter prepared you for the third Quarter. If you lack experience and knowledge, you will not handle the things life will throw your way in this Quarter. Some of those things are car insurance, car note, mortgage, children, college tuition, a home, a spouse and definitely debt. If you weren't prepared, you're going to fold in Quarter three. If you lacked experience and if you lacked knowledge, now here comes real life and it will knock you off your feet. Game on the line now and you're going to fold. A lot of people don't understand that these moments develop your thinking. A lot of people in this Quarter are influenced by society's thoughts and perceptions and how they are. You have to navigate around a lot of the noises in society today. You have to learn the mate you choose is a partner based on the fact that they are projected to grow with you and make your life easier. If you weren't taught these things in the first and second Quarter, you will make poor decisions when choosing a mate. Helpmate and teamwork are taught from youth, how to sacrifice, how to be financially stable all are taught in the first and second Quarter - when you're a youth. People make bad decisions because they weren't taught how to properly handle life in the first and second Quarter. They were not taught how to transition from one Quarter to the next. If people are making poor decisions in the third Quarter, that means they weren't taught properly in the first and second Quarter. They struggle as an adult because they weren't taught how to transition from childhood to adulthood. Those childhood days of no cares, no responsibilities were there in the first Quarter but you now have to transition to adulthood. Many people are adults and acting as if they are still kids and still behaving young. This occurs because we did not handle the first and second Quarters effectively. Fear of growing old affects us and these are normal occurrences; financial stability scares us. The fear of getting older and the struggle to find a career proves to be some of the obstacles faced because there was no adequate preparation during the first two Quarters of life.

Certain things that can't be done any longer in the third Quarter are not acceptable and resemble behaviors in the first two Quarters. In this Quarter, we lend thoughts to the fourth Quarter - the older years, our older selves. We will have a miserable last Quarter if we do not give thought to our later life in the third Quarter. Thoughts on pension, retirement, life insurance and even death should be thought about and preparations made for that older us.

Some people don't want to grow up so they suffer from an Identity crisis in this Quarter. They refuse to accept that they will get to an older age. Help your older self-transition. You cannot live like you're going to live forever. You have to think of your older self, how have you prepared for your older self. If the right money decisions aren't made in this Quarter, you'll suffer in the 4th Quarter. Thinking your kids will take care of you in your 4th Quarter and not making plans to live comfortably is absolutely bad. A lot of people suffer in their fourth Quarter because a lot of bad decisions and lack of preparation took place in the first, second and third Quarters.

4th Quarter

In this Quarter, retirement is now upon us. In this season of life, you will either enjoy it to the maximum or be miserable. The only way to determine how great your fourth Quarter will be is to learn in the first three Quarters and live effectively in the first three Quarters. It's about making the right decisions and preparing for this Quarter.

Life is on the line now; all of your preparations have gotten you to this very moment. The fourth Quarter exposes everything you have done up until now. There is no more faking it, instead here we are Reality. The way you spend your fourth Quarter is dependent on what you did with the other three Quarters. Let your final Quarter be so grand that you go out with astounding greatness because you prepared well and embraced your last three Quarters.

Chapter 15
YOU

As I look back on many moments of my life, I wondered why so many times I was challenged and had my back up against the wall, why I felt like I didn't want to move on, why I felt like giving or like I wasn't good enough. Now I realized that someone was watching me the entire time, further, I realized it was YOU. I used to always think I was alone, crying in a corner by myself, stressed out and aggravated, not realizing I had a purpose. It was YOU. You showed me I was meant to do bigger things, but yet still I kept questioning you, not realizing that you had a higher purpose and calling on my life. It was YOU. I had many battle scars from this journey called life, not realizing I was meant to go through this. I realized that as a warrior, as a man, as a conqueror, I had to go through the process in order to be humbled by you. I was made to understand that you are bigger than I. It was YOU. I used to always think why me? Why am I going through this not realizing that your purpose for my life was so big, therefore, I had to be processed.

Now, I use my voice to bring people to you, I adore you and I pray every day that you see me trying to be who you proposed me to be before I was even thought of. With this story you've allowed me, I will bring more people to you. It was YOU. I never realized that my words carry such great weight and are so meaningful, my words can impact so many lives. I took it for granted not realizing how great your purpose for my life was.

At times I saw myself stressed out and not wanting to be alive and taking it for granted. I took it for granted. To be honest, I didn't realize that every day was a blessing given to me to correct my wrongs and do things better. My intense immaturity caused me to challenge you, to challenge your greatness and to even challenge your influence in my life. There was a time when I thought you weren't really there, but boy did you show me. You used your love and compassion to prove to me that you do exist. In my saddest and darker days, you showed me you had my back even when I didn't have my own. Many days I spent alone wondering why. Some of my darkest moments were watching my mother struggle and couldn't afford certain things for me and many siblings, yet a way was made. It was YOU,

As I embark on this new chapter in life and I'm seeing that you have called me, I just want you to know that I need you to come with me. I don't want to forget what I've been through. I don't take life for granted, I'm grateful. I understand life more now than I ever did before and I know it's not about me. I used to think everything was about me and it should be easier for me. I used to feel sorry for myself. I used to feel like no one knew what I went through. Sometimes we evaluate people's lives but we don't understand what they're going through. A lot of people are fighting battles with themselves, to the naked eye they look like they got it together. That was me, fighting within myself but not showing it to anyone.

You made me know that I can call on you at any time and you'll be there. Truth be told, I'm never going back, I'll never look back. I don't want to stumble going forward by looking backward. I'm just asking you to watch over me. Please know I'm grateful. I'm no longer who I used to be. Our past can be whatever it was, but it's vital to get over our past. I was a very broken young man who thought I was an adult. I was very hurt and broken and emotional. I was really hurt but you showed me unconditional love. I used to wonder why, but now I see why. It was YOU. You knew what you wanted from me but I was scared to take on the responsibilities, and that was the problem. I was the problem. I traded the me, I traded the I for you.

Now that I know you, I don't need to call on a man. You showed me I can call on you because you are more than able. I don't fear walking in your name, I don't fear people knowing I have a relationship with you, I don't fear what people think about me. I fear no more. I feel sorry for those who don't know you because of the things you have done with my life and because of the powerful nature you have. I'm grateful and honored to even get this responsibility. Truth be told, to know you in of itself is a blessing. To have a relationship with you is even more of a blessing. I will never take anything for granted because you can make anything happen and you've done it with my life. In these chapters of this book, this is me speaking to me. I was a broken little boy who met you and now I realize believing in you, anything is possible. As I understand this, things have changed. I no longer point a finger because I realized that you give your hardest battles to your strongest soldiers, your toughest warriors. You ensure that by the time I receive a blessing, I'll know it was YOU. I've learnt something interesting about you, you don't sit in the heavens and prepare blessings for people, you prepare people for the blessings. Now I know you prepared me for the blessings. When I look back on my life, I realize I wasn't ready for these blessings I now have. Had you given them to me back then I would have made a mess of it. To whom much is given much is required. I now understand that every day is a blessing that I get to wake up. Every day we get up we should give thanks that we were able to even wake up. It is a blessing to have another day to live right. YOU clearly saw the reason and the purpose. I was angry, I was bitter, I was scorned - no one could feel my pain - growing up fatherless produced pain and anger. Watching my mother struggle was painful, I always wanted to protect, and I noticed you made me a protector. I will defend the weak for People who can't defend themselves. I noticed that's how you created me, but it was YOU. YOU showed me who I needed to be, you gave me purpose, you gave me reason, life and understanding. And now with these words, I tell you

135

every day I will never ever take you for granted. It is a blessing to wake up every day knowing you have life and that's the greatest blessing. I just wanted you to know that I will forever live for you. I am forever grateful that you have called and provided purpose to me and I will never forget that it was YOU - the giver of life. In honor of my Heavenly Father – my Savior, my Lord – YOU.

CPSIA information can be obtained
at www.ICGtesting.com
Printed in the USA
LVHW081535121222
735062LV00016B/1591